*Kena Upanishad
and Commentary*

By
Charles Johnston

Copyright © 2020 Lamp of Trismegistus. All rights reserved. No part of this publication may be reproduced or transmitted in any form or by any means, electronic or mechanical, including photocopying, recording, or by any information storage and retrieval system, without permission in writing from Lamp of Trismegistus. Reviewers may quote brief passages.

ISBN: 978-1-63118-491-8

Esoteric Classics:
Eastern Studies

Other Books in this Series and Related Titles

Isha Upanishad and Commentary by Charles Johnston (978-1-63118-490-1)

Katha Upanishad and Commentary by Charles Johnston (978-1-63118-493-2)

Prashna Upanishad and Commentary by Charles Johnston (978-1-63118-494-9)

Atma Bodha & Tattva Bodha by Adi Shankara &c (978-1-63118-401-7)

The Crest-Jewel of Wisdom by Adi Shankara (978-1-63118-475-8)

Catholicism, Yoga and Hinduism by Hartmann &c (978-1-63118-478-9)

Yoga, Hatha-Yoga and Raja-Yoga by Annie Besant (978-1-63118-476-5)

The Tree of Wisdom by Nagarjuna (978-1-63118-470-3)

The Path of Light: A Manual of Maha-Yana Buddhism (978-1-63118-471-0)

Buddhist Psalms by Shinran (978-1-63118-465-9)

Tao Te Ching & Commentary by Lao Tzu & C Johnston (978-1-63118-495-6)

The Hymns of Hermes by G. R. S. Mead (978-1-63118-405-5)

The Golden Verses of Pythagoras: Five Translations (978-1-63118-479-6)

Gnosis of the Mind by G. R. S. Mead (978-1-63118-408-6)

The Hymn of Jesus by G. R. S. Mead (978-1-63118-492-5)

The Book of the Watchers by Enoch (978-1-63118-416-1)

The Secrets of Enoch by Enoch (978-1-63118-449-9)

The Gospel of the Nativity of Mary by St. Matthew (978-1-63118-448-2)

Clairvoyance and Psychic Abilities by A Besant &c (978-1-63118-403-1)

A Collection of Early Writings on Astral Travel (978-1-63118-477-2)

The Sepher Yetzirah and the Qabalah by M P Hall (978-1-63118-481-9)

Audio versions are also available on Audible, Amazon and Apple

Table of Contents

Introduction...7

Kena Upanishad
Translated by Charles Johnston...9

"By Whom?"
Commentary on the Kena Upanishad
By Charles Johnston...17

Cena Upanishad
Translated by Raja Ram Mohun Roy...45

INTRODUCTION

The word "esoteric" can be difficult to define. Esotericism in general can be seen less as a system of beliefs and more as a category, which encompasses numerous, different systems of beliefs. It's a bit of juxtaposition, since the word "esoteric" indicates something that few people know about, while the term itself broadly covers numerous philosophies, practices, areas of study and belief systems.

In a greater sense, Esotericism acts as a storehouse for secret knowledge, which is often considered ancient *(by tradition, if not by fact)*, passed down from generation to generation, in private. At various times in history, simply possessing the knowledge of some of these subjects, was considered illegal and a jailable offence, if discovered. This usually included such general topics as Alchemy, Pharmacology, Qabalah, Hermeticism, Occultism, Ceremonial Magic, Astrology, Divination, Rosicrucianism and so on. Collectively, these areas of study were often referred to as the esoteric sciences.

Sometimes, the outer garment of a subject isn't esoteric, while what is hidden beneath it, is. As an example, Freemasonry isn't necessarily esoteric by nature (at *least not anymore)*, but certain signs, passwords and handshakes given to the candidate during their initiation, are in fact, esoteric, in the sense that they are hidden from the general public.

Today, in the twenty-first century, such topics are readily available at bookstores across the country, and numerous mainsteam publishers offer beginners guides and coffee-table volumes on many of these subjects, intended for mass appeal. Books like *"The Secret"* have turned previously arcane topics into household knowledge. All that being the case, however, it isn't to say that there still aren't buried secrets to uncover, ancient wisdom being ignored and forgotten mysteries to be explored. In fact, it is often that we are only able to further our own studies by standing on the shoulders of these disappearing giants.

Lamp of Trismegistus is doing its part to help preserve humanity's esoteric history by making some of these classics available to those students who are seeking to unearth the knowledge of these ancient colossi.

So, be sure to check other titles from our *Esoteric Classics* series, as well as our *Occult Fiction, Theosophical Classics, Foundations of Freemasonry Series, Supernatural Fiction, Paranormal Research Series, Studies in Buddhism* and our *Christian Apocrypha Series.* You can also download the audio versions of most of these titles from Amazon, Apple or Audible, for learning on the go.

KENA UPANISHAD

Translated by Charles Johnston

By whom impelled flies the forward-impelled Mind? By whom compelled does the First Life go forth? By whom impelled is this Voice that they speak? Who, in sooth, is the Bright One who compels sight and hearing?

That which they call the Hearing of hearing, the Mind of mind, the Voice of voice, that is the Life of life, the Sight of sight. Setting this free, the Wise, going forth from this world, become immortal.

Sight goes not thither, nor does voice go thither, nor mind. We have not seen, nor do we know, how one may transmit the understanding of this; for this is other than the known, other than the unknown also.

Thus have we heard from those who were before us, who have declared this unto us.

That which by voice is not spoken, that through whose power voice is spoken; that, verily, know thou as the Spirit, the Eternal, not this which here they honour and serve.

That which does not think through the power of the mind; that by which, they have declared, the mind is thought; that, verily, know thou as the Spirit, the Eternal, not this which here they honour and serve.

That which does not see through the power of sight; that by which he perceives sights; that, verily, know thou as the Spirit, the Eternal, not this which here they honour and serve.

That which does not hear through the power of hearing; that through whose power hearing is heard here; that, verily, know thou as the Spirit, the Eternal, not this which here they honour and serve.

That which does not live through the power of the life-breath; that through whose power the life-breath lives; that, verily, know thou as the Spirit, the Eternal, not this which here they honour and serve.

If thou thinkest: I know It well, little, indeed, of a truth, knowest thou that form of the Eternal—that form which thou art, that form which is in the Divine Powers; but if thou sayest: It is to be searched for and sought out, then I think It is known of thee.

He who says: I think not that I know It well, nor do I not know It—he, indeed, knows It. He who says: I know It, knows It not; he who thinks: I know It not, he knows It.

Of whom It is not understood, of him It is understood; of whom It is understood, he knows It not. It is uncomprehended of those who comprehend; It is comprehended of those who comprehend It not.

When It is known through illumination which turns toward It, and so is understood, then he who thus knows It, finds immortality. Through that Supreme Self he finds valour; through illumination he finds immortality.

If he has come to the knowledge of It in this present life, this is the supreme good. If he has not come to a knowledge of It, great is his loss, his fall. Searching for, and discerning It in all things that are, sages, going forth from this world, become immortal.

The Eternal, verily, won a victory for the Bright Powers. In the victory of That, of the Eternal, the Bright Powers magnified themselves. They, considering, said: Of us, verily, is this victory; of us, verily, is this might, said they.

That Eternal knew this thought of theirs. To them, verily, That manifested Itself. They knew It not. What apparition is this? said they.

They spoke to the Fire-god: Thou All-permeating, discover thou what this apparition is! said they.

Be it so! said he.

The Fire-god ran up to That.

That said to him: Who art thou?

The Fire-god, verily, am I! said he. The All-permeating am I!

If that be so, what valour is in thee? said That.

Even this all can I burn up, whatever there be, here in the world! said he.

Before him That laid down a blade of grass.

Burn this! said That.

He went forward toward it with all swiftness. He was not able to burn it.

From That, verily, he turned back.

I have not been able to discover what that apparition is! said he.

And so they spoke to the Wind-god: Thou Wind-god, discover thou what this apparition is! said they.

Be it so! said he.

The Wind-god ran up to That.

That said to him: Who art thou?

The Wind-god, verily, am I! said he. He who rests in the Mother am I!

If that be so, what valour is in thee? said That.

Even this all can I take up, whatever there be, here in the world! said he.

Before him That laid down a blade of grass.

Take up this! said That.

He went forward toward it with all swiftness. He was not able to take it up.

From That, verily, he turned back.

I have not been able to discover what that apparition is! said he.

And so they spoke to the Sky-lord: Thou Might-possessor, discover thou what this apparition is! said they.

Be it so! said he.

The Sky-lord ran up to That. That vanished from before him.

The Sky-lord there, verily, in the shining ether, came upon a Woman greatly radiant, Uma, daughter of the Snowy Mountain.

To her the Sky-lord spoke: What is this apparition? said he.

She spoke: The Eternal, verily! said she. In the victory of That ye were magnifying yourselves, said she.

From her, verily, he knew: It is the Eternal.

Therefore, verily, these Bright Powers stand in rank above the other Bright Powers, namely, the Fire-god, the Wind-god, the Sky-lord; for they touched That most nearly. And because he first knew that It is the Eternal, therefore the Sky-lord surpasses in rank the other Bright Powers; for he touched That most nearly, he first knew That, saying, It is the Eternal.

Of That, this is the teaching: That flashed forth from the lightning, like the twinkling of an eye. This concerns the celestial Powers.

Now, as concerns the Self: To That, intelligence approaches; and through That, the will constantly remembers That. This, verily, is named adoration of That; as adoration of That, it is to be approached with reverence. He who knows That thus, to him all beings are subject in loving obedience.

Thou hast said: Master, tell the Upanishad, the secret teaching! The Upanishad is declared to thee; we have, of a truth, declared the Upanishad concerning the Eternal; for this Upanishad, fervour, control, holy work are the support; the Vedas are its members; truth is its abode.

He who rightly knows this secret teaching, putting away darkness and sin, in the unending heavenly world which is to be won he stands firm, he stands firm.

"BY WHOM?"

KENA Upanishad

Translated from the Sanskrit with an Interpretation

By whom impelled flies the forward-impelled Mind? By whom compelled does the First Life go forth? By whom impelled is this Voice that they speak? Who, in sooth, is the Bright One who compels sight and hearing?

That which they call the Hearing of hearing, the Mind of mind, the Voice of voice, that is the Life of life, the Sight of sight. Setting this free, the Wise, going forth from this world, become immortal.

Sight goes not thither, nor does voice go thither, nor mind. We have not seen, nor do we know, how one may transmit the understanding of this; for this is other than the known, other than the unknown also.

Thus have we heard from those who were before us, who have declared this unto us.

That which by voice is not spoken, that through whose power voice is spoken; that, verily, know thou as the Spirit, the Eternal, not this which here they honour and serve.

That which does not think through the power of the mind; that by which, they have declared, the mind is thought; that, verily, know thott as the Spirit, the Eternal, not this which here they honour and serve.

That which does not see through the power of sight; that by which he perceives sights, that, verily, know thou as the Spirit, the Eternal, not this which here they honour and serve.

That which does not hear through the power of hearing; that through whose power hearing is heard here; that, verily, know thou as the Spirit, the Eternal, not this which here they honour and serve.

That which does not live through the power of the life-breath; that through whose power the life-breath lives; that, verily, know thou as the Spirit, the Eternal, not this which here they honour and serve.

There appear to be two fundamental thoughts in this passage from the beginning of the Upanishad "By Whom?"

The first thought is the character of the Spiritual Man, whom the Upanishads elsewhere call "the Man within, in the Heart"; that is, in the inner, spiritual nature.

The second thought is the immediate relation, the entire dependence of the Spiritual Man on the universal Divine Being, here called Brahma, "the Spirit, the Eternal, the Great Breath." Not only is the Spiritual Man dependent upon the Divine Being, but each and every power of the Spiritual Man depends upon, and draws its being from, the corresponding power of the Divine Being. This is the meaning of Paul's words: "in Him we live, and move, and have our being."

While these two thoughts are fundamentally one, being two sides of the same reality, it may be simpler to consider them separately.

To begin with the second verse: "That which they call the Hearing of hearing, the Mind of mind, the Voice of voice, that is the Life of life, the Sight of sight. Setting this free, the Wise, going forth from this world, become immortal."

Here, it is a question of the Sight, Hearing, Life-breath, Voice, Mind of the Spiritual Man, "the Man within, in the Heart," on the one hand, and the sight, hearing, life-breath, voice, mind of the outer personality, on the other. The Wise, the disciples, who set free the Spiritual Man, drawing him steadily forth "like the pith from a reed," from the meshes of the personal man, when they go forth from this world, become immortal.

The same thing is beautifully expressed in Katha Upanishad:

"When this lord of the body, standing within the body, departs; when he goes forth free from the body, what is left?"

The phrase, "the Sight of sight, the Hearing of hearing," recalls a kindred passage in Brihad Aranyaka Upanishad:

"The Spirit sees not; yet seeing not, he sees. For the energy that dwelt in sight cannot cease, because it is everlasting. But there is no other besides the Spirit, or separate from him, for him to see.

"The Spirit smells not; yet smelling not, he smells. For the energy that dwelt in the power of smell cannot cease, because it is everlasting. But there is nothing else besides the Spirit, or separate from him, for him to smell.

"The Spirit tastes not; yet tasting not, he tastes. For the energy that dwelt in taste cannot cease, because it is everlasting. But there is nothing else besides the Spirit, or separate from him, for him to taste.

"The Spirit speaks not; yet speaking not, he speaks. For the energy that dwelt in speech cannot cease, because it is everlasting. But there is nothing else, besides the Spirit, or separate from him, for him to speak to.

"The Spirit hears not; yet hearing not, he hears. For the energy that dwelt in hearing cannot cease, because it is everlasting. But there is nothing else besides the Spirit, or separate from him, for him to hear.

"The Spirit thinks not; yet thinking not, he thinks. For the energy that dwelt in thinking cannot cease, because it is everlasting. But there is nothing else besides the Spirit, or separate from him, for him to think of.

"The Spirit touches not; yet touching not, he touches. For the energy that dwelt in touch cannot cease, because it is everlasting. But there is nothing else besides the Spirit, or separate from him, for him to touch.

"The Spirit knows not; yet knowing not, he knows. For the energy that dwelt in knowing cannot cease, because it is everlasting. But there is nothing else besides the Spirit, or separate from him, for him to know."

Here again, we are concerned with the two sides of the same reality: on the one hand, the Spiritual Man, whose powers are formed of the essence, the energy, within the external powers; and, on the other hand, the unified Eternal Spirit, of which it cannot be said that it "sees, hears, knows," since there is no other being, separate from it, for it to see, hear, know. Nevertheless, within that Eternal Spirit dwell the essences, the energies, of all the powers; and from these centres of power, of spiritual energy, in the Eternal Spirit, are directly derived the different powers of the Spiritual Man.

Exactly the same thought appears to underlie the four unnumbered rules at the beginning of *Light on the Path*.

One may, perhaps, be permitted to add, within parentheses, a few words which will bring this out; premising, at the same time, that the full meaning goes much deeper, as is shown by the Author's Comments on these unnumbered rules.

If, then, it be permitted to add certain words, these rules would read thus:

"Before the (inner) eyes can see the (outer eyes) must be incapable of tears. Before the (inner) ear can hear (the outer ear) must have lost its sensitiveness. Before the (inner) voice can speak in the presence of the Masters (the outer voice) must have lost the power to wound. Before the soul (the Spiritual Man) can stand in the presence of the Masters its feet must be washed in the blood of the heart (through the purification of the whole personal nature)."

These parallels would seem to make sufficiently clear the thought of the Spiritual Man, the "lord of the body, standing within the body."

Yet the more vital side of the matter still remains to be emphasized: namely, that the Spiritual Man is not for a moment self-subsistent or self-dependent, but, moment by moment, draws his life-breath and the life of every one of his powers directly from the Eternal, the Spirit, the Great Breath.

And the whole life and development of the Spiritual Man depends on the practical realization of this moment to moment dependence on the Great Spirit; therefore the Upanishads are full of the Eternal.

With the sense of the overshadowing, over-ruling Eternal as guide, we may now take up the separate verses of the Upanishad "By Whom?" in the attempt to make their meaning clearer.

To the question: "By whom impelled flies the forward-impelled Mind?" the answer is: The Mind is impelled forward, impelled into objective life, by the Eternal; by that power, that ray of the Eternal, which may be called the Mind of the Eternal, the Mind of God; not in the general sense of the whole Logos, but in the special sense of that ray or principle of the Logos, which has the nature of Mind, and of which the human mind, and the mind in other living beings, is the ray, the manifestation.

In the same way, the answer to the second question: "By whom compelled does the First Life go forth?" is, that the compelling power which sends the first life, the ruling vital breath, into manifestation, is the Life-principle in the Eternal, the principle corresponding to the vital principle in human and other life; or rather, the principle which is the source and fountain of that life, and to which that life corresponds.

Similarly, the answer to the next question: "By whom impelled is this Voice that they speak?" is that this Voice, which means not only the actual power of speech, but the energizing, creative force which lies within and behind speech, and to which speech owes whatever it possesses of compelling force, is the ray, the representative of a like primal power or ray in the Eternal: that special power which has given the name Logos, "the Word," to the whole Being of the manifested Eternal.

The question: "Who, in sooth, compels sight and hearing?" may be answered in the same way. There is the primal power, the source and fountain head of these two forms of perception, in the manifested Eternal. These rays come down and manifest themselves in us, and in other living things, as the sight and hearing that we are familiar with, the ordinary perceptive powers which make use of the eyes and ears as their instruments.

We have, therefore, three groups or levels of these powers: first, their primal essence and source in the manifested Eternal; second, their manifestation in the Spiritual Man, the immortal, indicated in the second verse of the Upanishad; and, third, their everyday manifestation in the outer man. And one may conceive direct lines of connection, originating in each power of the Eternal; passing through the corresponding power of the Spiritual Man and continued to the outer power of the personal man, the eye, the ear, and so on.

Further, it would be wise to think of the Spiritual Man in two aspects, or, one might express it, at two stages. The first is the primal, ideal stage, which one might liken to an outline drawing of the future Spiritual Man. The second is the Spiritual Man, rendered fully conscious and individual by the transfer to him of the centred consciousness developed in the outer personality.

This transfer of the centred consciousness to the Spiritual Man is indicated in the first section of the second part of Katha Upanishad:

"The Self-Being pierced the openings outwards; hence one looks outward, not within himself. A wise man looked towards the Self with reverted sight, seeking deathlessness."

In this "reversion," this transfer of consciousness to the Spiritual Man, there are two principal elements: detachment from the outer, so constantly urged in the *Bhagavad Gita*, and recollection or one-pointed concentration, of which Patanjali has so much to say.

This phrase from Katha Upanishad may very well be taken as the answer to the question: "By whom impelled flies the forward-impelled Mind? . . . Who, in sooth, compels sight and hearing?" The answer is: The Self-Being, the manifested Logos.

We come now to the third verse: "Sight goes not thither, nor does voice go thither, nor mind. . . ."

It is a question of making known, so far as that can be known, the nature and being of the Eternal, the Spirit, the Great Breath.

That Spirit cannot be seen by the eyes; it is not externally visible as are natural objects. Nor can it be described in words, nor thought of by the external mind, the mental machine; because the mind-machine and the words it uses have both been developed to meet and describe external conditions of manifested things. Therefore they cannot be adequately used to describe or discern the Unmanifest.

The Spirit, the Eternal, is other than the known: other than what is perceived and known by the external senses and the mind-machine. But, since this Spirit is, as we have seen, the source and fountain head of each of these powers, and of the mind also, the Spirit cannot be regarded as alien and infinitely remote. It is, therefore, different from the unknown also.

Concerning the transmission of the knowledge of this, we should always keep in mind the fundamental fact that all Consciousness is ultimately one. There is no absolute chasm, no complete solution of continuity, between my personal consciousness at this moment, and the infinite Consciousness of the Eternal. We are not isolated lives, we are not islands of consciousness; or we are islands only in the sense that all islands are connected together, beneath the ocean.

If it were not for this connection, existing at this moment, existing everlastingly, the matter of our salvation, our liberation, would be hopeless. The chasm could never be bridged.

But the link is there, the connection is there, the bridge is there; it is only a question of our passing over the bridge; and detachment and recollection, which take advantage of the divine forces stretched out toward us, will carry us across.

The knowledge of the Eternal, therefore, could never be transmitted from one isolated soul to another. But, since the Eternal is in both, no such transmission is needed. What is needed is the direction of the attention to what is already there: the divine light within the heart. And one may say that the whole of the Upanishads exist, simply to direct our attention to that "inward light."

The remaining sentences of the passage translated are intended to awaken the intuition of that inward light, to direct our attention to it, to make us more vividly aware of its presence and nature.

The inward light, the divine power within, is "that through whose power voice is spoken." For speech is an expression, a using, of both understanding and will; and understanding and will are manifestations of the inward divine life. And it should be kept in mind, as pointed out before, that "voice" means, not so much uttered speech, as the divine and magical force within speech and manifested by speech; the creative power represented by the pentecostal tongues of flame.

That divine, creative power, therefore, the power which lies behind uttered speech, is to be known as the Spirit; not "this which here they honour and serve."

This last phrase is interpreted by the traditional commentaries as indicating the popular divinities, Agni, Vayu,

Indra, and the rest; personified rays of the infinite Spirit, the Great Breath.

But we may take the matter more intimately: "this which here they honour and serve" fairly represents the personal self, whom most of us do so inveterately honour and serve.

It is a question, therefore, of detachment; a question of changing self-love into love of the Divine; of transferring the consciousness from the outer man to the Spiritual Man.

But here it is well to keep in mind what was said at the outset: the vital fact about the Spiritual Man is, that he lives and breathes through the life of the Eternal in him. Not for an instant may he be thought of as separate and independent; his very being depends, from instant to instant, upon the Eternal, and upon ceaseless obedience to the laws of the Eternal. This immediate dependence of the Spiritual Man on the Eternal is the foremost fact of his being.

For the disciple, this will mean that his inner life is sustained from moment to moment by the life of his Master, who embodies and focuses the Eternal for him; the life-breath of the disciple will be unceasing obedience to the will of the Eternal, expressed through the will of his Master.

This will not mean passivity. Far from it, since the will of the Eternal is a divine, creative will. Therefore obedience to the divine will, the Master's will, and response to that will, means the gradual exercise of divine, creative power, but always in entire compliance with the plan of the Master, the Eternal.

The Upanishad goes on to fix our attention upon the inner Spirit within each of our powers: sight, hearing, life-breath, mind. The purpose is recollection, inwardness, to be brought about through detachment and concentration; thus gradually transferring to the Spiritual Man the life-forces previously squandered upon the outer man, and at the same time constantly keeping alive the intuition and recognition of the Eternal, the Spirit, the Great Breath, as the source and inspiration and home of the Spiritual Man.

II

If thou thinkest: I know It well, little, indeed, of a truth, knowest thou that form of the Eternal—that form which thou art, that form which is in the Divine Powers; but if thou sayest: It is to be searched for and sought out, then I think It is known of thee.

He who says: I think not that I know It well, nor do I not know It—he, indeed, knows It. He who says: I know It, knows It not; he who thinks: I know It not, he knows It.

Of whom It is not understood, of him It is understood; of whom It is understood, he knows It not. It is uncomprehended of those who comprehend; It is comprehended of those who comprehend It not.

When It is known through illumination which turns toward It, and so is understood, then he who thus knows It, finds immortality. Through that Supreme Self he finds valour; through illumination he finds immortality.

If he has come to the knowledge of It in this present life, this is the supreme good. If he has not come to a knowledge of It, great is his loss, his fall. Searching for, and discerning It in all things that are, sages, going forth from this world, become immortal.

The subject of these enigmatical sentences is the Eternal, the Supreme Self of all beings. And in this second name of that ineffable Mystery one may, perhaps, find a way to an understanding of these riddles.

Let us begin by realizing that Spiritual Life, the Eternal, the Supreme Self cannot be known by the lower, external mind; the marvelous piece of machinery which we have through ages developed, to deal with material objects and conditions; the mind which determines the nature of things external by measuring them, by comparing, by weighing one against another; the mind on which we depend in the practical things of daily life.

This wonderful piece of machinery has been specialized for exactly these practical ends, and has a certain quite limited scope. It can weigh and measure and compare. It can never, because of its very nature, tell us about the real nature of anything; can never tell us what anything really is. This limitation is of the essence of its nature, because it is of no practical value to us, in our daily lives, to know the real nature of things, any more than it would be of practical value to rabbits to know the botanical classification of the different grasses. Rabbits can get along quite well with a relative knowledge, the knowledge of the flavour and wholesomeness of different green things; any further knowledge would be a useless encumbrance.

So in us the lower, external mind, the mind which looks outward upon external nature, needs only relative knowledge of things, and not a knowledge of what they really are. It was brought into being for just that purpose, and is, by its nature, strictly limited to that function.

But there is within us another power, the beginning of which is intuition. Bergson, who has approached nearest to the Eastern Wisdom in his consideration of these high problems, rightly says that this power, intuition, is not a machine which measures and compares, but is the representative in us, in our inmost being, of the Infinite Life; is at once the Infinite Life and the most real element of our being; and, because it is this, intuition can give us some perception, some experience, of Infinite Being; not through a process of outward viewing, of weighing and measuring and comparing, but through direct spiritual self-consciousness, through being that which we know.

The external mind, therefore, cannot know Life, the Eternal, the Supreme Self of all beings. But, through a reversal of the tendency of our lives, through a withdrawing of ourselves from the entanglements of external things and a turning inward and upward within ourselves, we can awaken intuition, we can reach spiritual self-consciousness; we can begin to realize the Eternal, because the Eternal is the very essence of that new part of ourselves which we have awakened to consciousness; or, to speak more correctly, that part of ourselves to a consciousness of which we have awakened. We begin to know the Eternal by awaking to a realization that we are of the Eternal, that we are in the Eternal; that the Eternal is that within us, which both knows and is known. It is a process, not of mental measurement and comparison, but of spiritual self-consciousness.

A part of the lasting tragedy of human life is this: The lower, external mind not only cannot understand the real nature of things, the real nature of the Infinite Life, the Eternal, and our relation with that Life; the lower mind cannot even recognize that knowledge of this kind exists, nor is such knowledge of even the slightest interest to the lower mind. It will of itself never even ask the question.

But, in virtue of the divinity within mankind, in virtue of the spiritual stature and endowment which renders his inner nature to some degree self-conscious, there is, within him, some measure of intuition. And this first glimmer of intuition does ask the infinite question; does concern itself with the reality of things, does seek to sound the infinitudes. This it does, because it is itself of the essence of the Infinite.

Intuition, therefore, puts the question concerning things infinite. The lower, external mind catches the reflection of this question from the intuition above and within; seizes on the question, and strains its powers to find the answer. This would seem to be the motive and driving power of all rationalistic philosophies.

But, having undertaken this large task, the external mind carries with it its inherent limitations. It is not equipped, nor was it constructed, to perform work of this kind. Therefore, while straining at the task, the lower mind cannot accomplish it; it is fatally pursued by its inherent limitedness.

Seeking to unravel the secret of the external world, the lower mind discovers matter; discovers the elements that make up matter, defining these elements in terms of weight and measurement, and their interactions among themselves; discovers molecules within the elements, atoms within the molecules, ions or electrons within the atoms; and, at last, is as far from the ultimate solution as it was at the outset.

In exactly the same way, the lower mind measures the world and its girth; goes beyond the earth to the moon and sun and the whole solar system, measuring and weighing these; passes beyond the solar system to the starry hosts; and then, as before, comes to a halt; recognizes that it cannot conceive the universe either as having a boundary or as having no boundary. While ascertaining comparative measures and distances, it has learned nothing of realities. Everything is described in terms of something else; there is no finality, or possible finality.

Therefore all rationalistic philosophies end, and inevitably end, in agnosticism. That is the one logical conclusion to the search for knowledge in that way, by that instrument.

The tragedy, therefore, is this: That, having been inspired and set in motion by intuition, which alone puts the questions he seeks to answer, the rationalistic philosopher instantly turns his back upon intuition and commits the task to the lower mind, which is incapable of finding the answer. Having begun with intuition, he should go on with intuition; pressing with his whole life-force and energy in that direction, he will find it possible, with the co-operation of Divine Powers which are waiting to help him, to arouse intuition into a flame of light, a perceptive power which really knows the Eternal, because it is itself of the essence of the Eternal; a power which will know the Eternal as Infinite, Immortal; knowing this by the direct experience of spiritual consciousness; and, further, recognizing this radiant inner Life as the Supreme Self, the Supreme Life of all beings. Spiritual intuition recognizes that Life is infinite; in knowing, it therefore at the same time knows that it can never be completely known; that it can never be fully comprehended, girdled by knowledge. This recognition comes as an early experience of intuition, and is testified to by all, in all times and lands, in whom spiritual intuition has awakened. Yet, recognizing that the Life is infinite, and never fully to be known, intuition at the same time recognizes a kindred infinity within its own being, and sees for itself the promise of an immortal, infinitely growing Light.

While the lower mind cannot lay hold on realities, nor grasp what belongs to intuition, to spiritual consciousness, nevertheless the lower mind is not in underlying substance different from intuition. It is rather a part of intuition, but crystallized, set, specialized; just as the hand is specialized, from the general substance of the body, for a limited use. But the specialized organ pays the penalty of its specialization and cannot re-become the general substance. A bird's wing is, in reality, a five-fingered hand specialized for flight; but it cannot rebecome a hand. The hoof of a horse is a still more specialized five-fingered hand; it can become neither hand nor wing.

But the important thing is, that the general substance can take this or that special form, because it has in it all that will be developed in either special form. So the intuition has in it the essence of all the specialized forms and means of knowledge which are crystallized in the lower mind. It is a noetic power with infinite power of application.

We shall miss the real purpose of these considerations if we think of them as applying only to forms and means of knowledge. The real application is to being rather than knowing only. It is not so much a question of spiritual knowledge as of spiritual life; of the awakened spiritual will, rather than of new modes of knowing.

It is not enough to do what has been suggested: to turn backward and inward the perceptive powers; we must turn ourselves backward and inward, renouncing not so much the lower mind, as the whole life of the lower self, with the whole body of corrupt inclinations and tendencies that make it up. It is a question of repentance, conversion, redemption through the divine grace of Spiritual Powers.

But the life of the lower self is tenaciously defended by the lower mind, which is the acute, resourceful, obedient servitor of the lower will. Therefore we can make the conflict easier by solving, to some degree, the problem of the lower mind, thus weakening its prestige and shaking its despotic sway. This is a means, a partial means only. The great battle must be fought out in the moral nature, with the light and help of Spiritual Powers; Powers which are constrained by the infinite Unity to lend their help. And the name of that constraint is Divine Love.

Keeping these general considerations in mind, it will be less difficult to read the riddle of the sentences translated:

If thou thinkest: I know the Infinite Eternal well, completely, that Eternal Life of which thou art, of which the Divine Powers are, undivided parts,—little dost thou know. It is to be searched for and sought after in the inner, spiritual nature, which is to be entered by the door of sacrifice and aspiration, with the help of the Divine Powers; then, indeed, it will be known.

He who says: I think not that I know it well, so as completely to comprehend and girdle it with my knowledge; nor do I not know it, since it is the essence of my spiritual nature, and therefore my innermost consciousness and will, he, indeed, knows the Eternal.

With these clues and examples, it will not be hard to read the ancient riddle.

The Eternal, verily, won a victory for the Bright Powers. In the victory of That, of the Eternal, the Bright Powers magnified themselves. They, considering, said: Of us, verily, is this victory; of us, verily, is this might, said they.

That Eternal knew this thought of theirs. To them, verily, That manifested Itself. They knew It not. What apparition is this! said they.

They spoke to the Fire-god: Thou AU-permeating, discover thou what this apparition is! said they.

Be it so! said he.

The Fire-god ran up to That. That said to him: Who art thou?

The Fire-god, verily, am I! said he. The All-permeating am I! If that be so, what valour is in thee! said That.

Even this all can I burn up, whatever there be, here in the world! said he.

Before him That laid down a blade of grass. Burn this! said That.

He went forward toward it with all swiftness. He was not able to burn it.

From That, verily, he turned back.

I have not been able to discover what that apparition is! said he. And so they spoke to the Wind-god: Thou Wind-god, discover thou what this apparition is! said they.

Be it so! said he.

The Wind-god ran up to That. That said to him: Who art thou?

The Wind-god, verily, am I! said he. He who rests in the Mother am I!

If that be so, what valour is in thee? said That.

Even this all can I take up, whatever there be, here in the world! said he.

Before him That laid down a blade of grass. *Take up this!* said That.

He went forward toward it with all swiftness. He was not able to take it up.

From That, verily, he turned back.

I have not been able to discover what that apparition is! said he. And so they spoke to the Sky-lord: *Thou Might-possessor, discover thou what this apparition is!* said they.

Be it so! said he.

The Sky-lord ran up to That. That vanished from before him.

The Sky-lord there, verily, in the shining ether, came upon a Woman greatly radiant, Uma, daughter of the Snowy Mountain.

To her the Sky-lord spoke: *What is this apparition?* said he.

She spoke: *The Eternal, verily!* said she. *In the victory of That ye were magnifying yourselves,* said she.

From her, verily, he knew: It is the Eternal.

The passage just translated is, perhaps, the most delicious bit of Sanskrit prose that has come down to us; fascinating in the great simplicity of its style, charming in its sense of humour.

It is, at the same time, one of the deepest passages in all the Upanishads, the profoundest books of the Eastern Wisdom.

We can, therefore, hope to discover only a part of its mystery, which is, indeed, the supreme mystery of the Eternal.

We can best seek the meaning of this splendidly vivacious piece of symbolism by translating certain sentences from a Vedanta catechism attributed to one of the great Masters of the Eastern Wisdom, Shankaracharya, who both edited and commented on the greater Upanishads, though the commentaries we have were probably written not by that Master but by some of his disciples.

The sentences are these:

The Supreme Self, attributing itself to, and becoming self-conscious in, the natural body, is called the All-pervading (Vishva, Vaishvanara).

The Supreme Self, attributing itself to, and becoming self-conscious in, the mental body, is called the Radiant (Taijasa).

The Supreme Self, attributing itself to, and becoming self-conscious in, the causal body (Karana sharira) is called the Illuminated (Prajna).

The Supreme Self (Atma) in its own form, is Infinite Being, Infinite Consciousness, Infinite Bliss.

There is, therefore, on the one hand, the Supreme Self, the Eternal. On the other hand, there are the three bodies, counting from below upward, the natural body, the mental body, the causal body. And, in each of these three bodies, there is the apparition, the presentment, of the Supreme Self: the self in that body. In the natural body is the vital, natural self; the self common to all living things, the all-permeating, all-pervading vital fire. In the mental body is the personal self, in the higher sense of personality, the personal man redeemed. In the causal body is the self of illumination, the permanent individuality, as distinguished from the true personality.

One might, perhaps, distinguish these three as the self of the ordinary man, the self of the full disciple, and the self of the Master.

This seems to be very closely the ground covered by the first, or microcosmic, meaning of our ancient parable.

The victory which the Eternal won for the Bright Powers would appear to be the victory of manifestation, of existence in manifested life.

This manifestation, like the unrolling of a curtain, is let down through the Three Worlds, the spiritual world, the mid-world and the natural world.

In the lowest of the three, the natural world, Life is manifested as the habitual self, perhaps it would be better to say, the vital self, in the natural body.

On its own plane, natural life, vitality, pervades all things and sets all things aflame with vital breath. Through that power, the whole natural universe moves and breathes and has its being.

But, faced with the mystery of Life, the natural self is impotent. Even a blade of grass presents an unconquerable enigma. The digestive powers even of a rabbit can consume the blade of grass. But the natural intelligence even of the wisest botanist cannot solve the ultimate problem of the blade of grass, the mystery of the being that is within it.

For the self of the mental body, which begins where reflective self-consciousness begins, but which fully disentangles itself from the natural self only when the disciple comes to full self-consciousness in the mental body, the ultimate mystery is equally impenetrable. The activity of the mental self, like the wind of heaven, sweeps to the uttermost bounds of visible space, only to be completely baffled. The intelligence of that self cannot take up even a blade of grass, and discern its final secret.

We come now to deep waters; waters considerably beyond the depth of the present interpreter. But, in the writings attributed to Shankaracharya, there is what would appear to be a clue. It is said there that the causal body has two aspects: on the one hand, it is the vesture of the illuminated consciousness of the Master, the immortal; on the other hand, the causal body, since it is the basis of individuality, and, therefore, of separate existence, of differentiation, is, in a sense, opposed to the Oneness of the Eternal. The heterogeneous cannot comprehend the homogeneous. The differentiated cannot comprehend the undifferentiated.

Looking at this from another point of view: Even when the disciple has attained to mastery, fully awakening the illuminated self-consciousness in the causal body, there appear to be two alternative ways open: He may either elect to enter Nirvana, which an august authority has called "a glorified selfishness"; or he may renounce his reward, and enter the gate of absolute sacrifice.

Only if he choose the second alternative, has he entered into the true mystery of the Eternal.

It would seem that there are in him the two counterbalancing tendencies: on the one hand, the causal body which, as the basis of separateness, is biased toward separate existence, individual Nirvana; on the other hand, the illuminated consciousness, the very light of the Eternal, inspiring him to renounce individual bliss and to throw his whole life and being into the continuing struggle of All that lives, the eternal warfare for spiritual victory.

But these are somewhat rash speculations, venturings into too deep water.

Besides its application to the microcosm, to sevenfold man, our ancient parable has also its macrocosmic side, referring to the same principles in their universal aspect, as principles of worlds and solar systems. This macrocosmic side is brought out in the passage which follows, and which completes this Upanishad:

Therefore, verily, these Bright Powers stand in rank above the other Bright Powers, namely, the Fire-god, the Wind-god, the Sky-lord; for they touched That most nearly. And because he first knew that It is the Eternal, therefore the Sky-lord surpasses in rank the other Bright Powers; for he touched That most nearly, he first knew That, saying, It is the Eternal.

Of That, this is the teaching: That flashed forth from the lightning, like the twinkling of an eye. This concerns the celestial Powers.

Now, as concerns the Self: To That, intelligence approaches; and through That, the will constantly remembers That . This, verily, is named adoration of That; as adoration of That, it is to be approached with reverence. He who knows That thus, to him all beings are subject in loving obedience.

Thou hast said: Master, tell the Upanishad, the secret teaching!

The Upanishad is declared to thee; we have, of a truth, declared the Upanishad concerning the Eternal; for this Upanishad, fervour, control, holy work are the support; the Vedas are its members; truth is its abode.

He who rightly knows this secret teaching, putting away darkness and sin, in the unending heavenly world which is to be won he stands firm, he stands firm.

We have, perhaps, in this last passage, the clue to the most mysterious personage in our ancient parable: Uma, daughter of the Snowy Mountain, Uma Haimavati.

In the later and more exoteric, but still mystical, tradition of India, Uma is the consort of Shiva, Third Person of the Trimurti, the Lord of mystical wisdom, whose name signifies the August, the Benign. It is, therefore, the hidden wisdom, personified as the child of the Himalaya, who reveals the Eternal.

Curiously, while the inner significance of the name of this Woman greatly radiant is lost in Sanskrit, it must have been clear in the older tongue which lies behind Sanskrit; for it remains in a group of younger Aryan tongues called Slavonic. Here, the root Um is the common word for intelligence.

Cosmic Intelligence, therefore, on the one hand, the divine power which has been called Cosmic Electricity; and, on the other, that spiritual intelligence in man, the first manifestation of which is intuition, which steadily grows, as we watch and worship, till it becomes the infinite Light, revealing the Supreme Eternal; such would seem to be the significance of Uma, daughter of the Snowy Mountain, consort of the mystic Lord.

Cena Upanishad

Translated By Raja Ram Mohun Roy

1st. Who is he [asks a pupil of his spiritual father,] under whose sole will the intellectual power makes its approach to *different objects?* Who is he under whose authority *breath*, the primitive *power in the body*, makes its operation? Who is he by whose direction language is regularly pronounced? And who is that immaterial being that applies vision and hearing *to their respective objects?*

2nd. He, [answers the spiritual parent,] who is the sense of the sense of hearing; the intellect of the intellect; the essential cause of language; the breath of breath; the sense of the sense of vision;— this is the Being *concerning whom you would* enquire. Learned men, having relinquished *the notion of self-independence and self-consideration from knowing the Supreme Understanding to be the sole source of sense*, enjoy everlasting beatitude after their departure from this world.

3rd. Hence no vision can approach him, no language can describe him, no intellectual power can compass or determine him. We know nothing of how the Supreme Being should be explained: he is beyond all that is within the reach of comprehension, and also beyond nature, which is above conception. Our ancient *spiritual parents* have thus explained him to us.

4th. He alone, who has never been described by language, and who directs language *to its meaning*, is the Supreme Being, and not any specified thing which men worship; know THOU this.

5th. He alone, whom understanding cannot comprehend, and who, as said *by learned men*, knows the real nature of understanding, is the Supreme Being, and not any specified thing which men worship; know THOU this.

6th. He alone, whom no one can conceive by vision, and by whose superintendence every one perceives the objects of vision, is the Supreme Being, and not any specified thing which men worship: know THOU this.

7th. He alone, whom no one can hear through the sense of hearing, and who knows the real nature of the sense of hearing, is the Supreme Being, and not any specified thing which men worship: know THOU this.

8th. He alone, whom no one can perceive through the sense of smelling, and who applies the sense of smelling *to its objects*, is the Supreme Being, and not any specified thing which men worship: know THOU this.

9th. If you [*continues the spiritual parent*], *from what I have stated*, suppose *and say* that "I know the Supreme Being thoroughly," you in truth know very little of the Omnipresent Being; and any conception of that Being which you limit to your powers of sense, is not only deficient, but also his description which you extend to the bodies of the celestial gods, is also imperfect; you consequently should enquire into the true knowledge of the Supreme Being. *To this the pupil replies*: "I perceive that *at this moment* I begin to know God."

10th. "Not that I suppose," *continues* he, "that I know God thoroughly, nor do I suppose that I do not know him at all: as, among us, he who knows the meaning of the above-stated assertion, is possessed of the knowledge respecting God; *viz*. "that I neither know him thoroughly, nor am entirely ignorant of him."

11th. [*The Spiritual Father again resumes*:] He who believes that he cannot comprehend God, *does* know him; and he who believes that he can comprehend God, *does not* know him: as men of perfect understanding acknowledge him to be beyond comprehension; and men of imperfect understanding suppose him to be within the reach of their simplest perception.

12th. The notion of the sensibility of bodily organs, *which are composed of insensible particles*, leads to the notion of God; which notion alone is accurate, and tends to everlasting happiness. Man gains, by self-exertion, the power of acquiring knowledge respecting God, and through the same acquisition he acquires eternal beatitude.

13th. Whatever person has, *according to the above stated doctrine*, known God, is really happy, and whoever has not known him is subjected to great misery. Learned men, having reflected on the Spirit of God extending over all moveable as well as immoveable creatures, after their departure from this world are absorbed into the Supreme Being.

In a battle between the celestial gods and the demons, God obtained victory over the latter, in favour of the former (*or properly speaking, God enabled the former to defeat the latter*); but, upon this victory being gained, the celestial gods acquired their respective dignities, and supposed that this victory and glory were entirely owing to themselves. The Omnipresent Being, having known their boast, appeared to them *with an appearance beyond description.*

They could not know what adorable appearance it was: they, *consequently,* said to fire, *or properly speaking, the* god of fire: "Discover thou, O god of fire, what adorable appearance this is." His reply was, "I shall." He proceeded fast to that adorable appearance, which asked him, "Who art thou?" He then answered, "I am fire, and I am the origin of the Ved;" *that is, I am a well-known personage.* The Supreme Omnipotence, upon being thus replied to, asked him *again,* "What power is in so celebrated a person as thou art?" He replied, "I can burn to ashes all that exists in the world." The Supreme Being then having laid a straw before him, said to him, "Canst thou burn this straw?" The god of fire approached the straw, but could not burn it, though he exerted all his power. He then *unsuccessfully* retired and *told the others,* "I have been unable to discover what adorable appearance this is." Now they all said to wind (*or properly to the god of wind*), "Discover thou, O god of wind, what adorable appearance this is." His reply was, "I shall." He proceeded fast to that adorable appearance, which asked him, "Who art thou?" He then answered, "I am wind, and I pervade unlimited space;" *that is, I am a well-known personage.* The Supreme Being, *upon being* thus replied to, asked him *again*, "What power is in so celebrated a person as thou art?" He replied, "I can uphold all that exists in the world." The Supreme Being then, having laid a straw before him, said to him, "Canst thou uphold this straw?" The god of wind approached the straw, but could not hold it up, though he exerted all his power. He then *unsuccessfully* retired *and told the others*, "I have been unable to discover what adorable appearance this is." Now they all said to the god of atmosphere, "Discover thou, O revered god of atmosphere, what adorable appearance this is." His reply was, "I shall," He proceeded fast to that adorable appearance, which vanished from his view. He met at the same spot a woman, *the goddess of instruction*, arrayed in golden robes in the shape of the most beautiful Uma. He asked, "What was that adorable appearance?" She replied, "It was the Supreme Being owing to whose victory you are all advanced to exaltation." The god of atmosphere, from her instruction, knew that it was the Supreme Being *that had appeared to them. He at first communicated that information to the gods of fire and of wind.* As the gods of fire, wind, and atmosphere had approached to the adorable appearance, and had perceived it, and also as they had known, prior *to the others*, that it was indeed God *that appeared to them*, they seemed to be superior to the other gods. As the god of atmosphere had approached to the adorable appearance, and perceived it, and also as he knew, prior to *every one of them*, that it was God *that appeared to them*, he seemed not only superior to every other god, but also, *for that reason*, exalted above the gods of fire and wind.

The foregoing is a divine figurative representation of the Supreme Being; meaning that in one instant he shines at once *over all the universe* like the illumination of lightning; and in another, that he disappears as quick as the twinkling of an eye. Again, it is represented *of the Supreme Being*, that *pure* mind conceives that it approaches to him as nearly as possible: Through the same pure mind the pious man thinks of him, and consequently application of the mind to him is repeatedly used. That God, *who alone in reality has no resemblance, and to whom the mind* cannot approach, is adorable by all living creatures; he is therefore called "*adorable*;" he should, *according to the prescribed manner*, be worshipped. All creatures revere the person who knows God in the manner thus described. The pupil *now says*, "Tell me, O Spiritual Father, the Upanishad or the principal part of the Ved." The *Spiritual Father makes this answer*, "I have told you the principal part of the Ved which relates to God alone, and, indeed told you the Upanishad, of which, austere devotion, control over the senses, performance of religious rites, and the remaining parts of the Ved, as well as those sciences that are derived from the Veds, are *only* the feet; and whose altar and support is truth." He who understands it as thus described, having relieved himself from sin, acquires eternal and unchangeable beatitude.

www.ingramcontent.com/pod-product-compliance
Lightning Source LLC
LaVergne TN
LVHW041500070426
835507LV00009B/727